Steck-Vaughn

Building Success

· IN THE WORKPLACE ·

R. Lois Teal

Consultant: Connie Eichhorn

Steck-Vaughn Company Adult Education Advisory Council

Donna Amstutz
Asst. Project Director
Northern Area Adult Education
  Service Center
Northern Illinois University
DeKalb, Illinois

Myra Baum
Adult Basic Education
New York, New York

Sharon K. Darling
President, National Center for
  Family Literacy
Louisville, Kentucky

Lonnie D. Farrell
Supervisor, Adult Special Programs
Los Angeles Unified School District
Los Angeles, California

Meredyth A. Leahy
Director of Continuing Education
Cabrini College
Radnor, Pennsylvania

Roberta Pittman
Director, Project C3 Adult
  Basic Education
Detroit Public Schools
Detroit, Michigan

Don Seaman
Professor of Adult Education
Texas A & M University
College Station, Texas

Jane B. Sellen
Supervisor, Adult Education
Western Iowa Tech Community
  College
Sioux City, Iowa

Elaine Shelton
President, Shelton Associates
Competency-Based Adult
  Education Consultant
Austin, Texas

Bobbie Walden
Coordinator, Community Education
Alabama Department of Education
Montgomery, Alabama

Steck-Vaughn Company

A Subsidiary of National Education Corporation

CONTENTS

About the Author

R. Lois Teal has a commitment of long standing to the cause of vocational education for students with special needs. A teacher for twenty-nine years in Cleveland, Ohio, and Houston, Texas, she was instrumental in the establishment of vocational programs at the local and state levels. Lacking adequate instructional materials, she began to write her own. She is the author of several curriculum guides and workbooks in the area of preparing students for job success. This book is evidence of her belief that "every person has worth and should be helped to develop his or her potential to the greatest degree."

Photography
Cover: © UNIPHOTO/Jim Olive
Bill Records
James Minor

ISBN 0-8114-4221-7

3 4 5 6 7 8 9 HG 95 94 93 92 91

BEAT THE CLOCK

*Is there a word in the list at left you don't know?
Look it up in the Glossary in the back of the book.*

STUDY WORDS

aides

alarm

appreciate

audio-visual

community

depend

equipment

operate

permits

program

projector

report

Al and Bert go to the community college. They work part-time at the college. They help the teachers with audio-visual machines. The teachers depend on them to run the machines.

Al and Bert set up the equipment and take it down after it has been used. The equipment must be put away in the audio-visual storage room. Al and Bert both know how to operate the machines. They have been audio-visual aides for a year.

One of Mrs. Wilson's classes meets on Tuesday and Thursday mornings at 7:30. Sometimes a film is shown to the students. A film was ordered this week.

Al and Bert were to set up the equipment and operate the projector. Both of them have special permits to enter the building early. They agreed to meet in front of the building at

7:15 the next morning. They wanted to be ready to start before the time for the program to begin.

Bert arrived at 7:10 and waited for Al. Al did not come. At 7:20 Bert hurried into the building to set up the screen and the projector. He was ready to show the film by 7:30.

Al came in as the program started. Bert asked Al to operate the projector so he could study. After the film was over, both boys put the equipment back in the audio-visual room.

"What happened to you?" asked Bert. "I waited for you until 7:20. Then I thought I better get everything ready to start."

"My alarm woke me up," said Al, "but I went back to sleep. I didn't wake up until almost seven o'clock. I hurried then! I'm sorry I was late."

"I really had to hurry," said Bert. "I didn't want the movie to start late. Mrs. Wilson might report us."

Mrs. Wilson came in to pick up the film. "Good morning," she said. "How did everything go this morning?"

"We made it fine," said Bert. "Here are the keys, Al. Lock the cabinet."

Mrs. Wilson said, "Thanks for getting up so early to show the film. I really appreciate it." She left.

"Why didn't you tell her I was late?" asked Al.

"I like to work with you," said Bert. "I think we work well together. I was afraid Mrs. Wilson might say something to our boss. We might not get to work together again."

"You mean you still want to work with me even though I was late?" asked Al.

"Just get here when you are supposed to next time," said Bert.

"Don't worry, I will," said Al.

For more information about this job, see PROJECTIONIST in the Dictionary of Job Descriptions at the back of this book.

A • THINGS TO TALK ABOUT

1. How many things in our lives are done by the clock

2. How you feel about programs that start late or people who are always late

3. Times when being late cannot be helped

4. Why Bert did not tell the teacher about Al being late

5. When it is and is not necessary to report others

B • QUESTIONS TO ANSWER

1. Why is it necessary for Al and Bert to be on time?

_____

2. Which person was late? _____

THE TOOLROOM MYSTERY

STUDY WORDS

attendant

clue

expensive

investigate

mechanic

pretend

repair

thief

toolroom

CHARACTERS

RAMONA, *the toolroom attendant*

MR. JOHNSON, *the service manager*

POLICE OFFICER

SETTING

The service department at a new car dealership. Ramona checks tools out to mechanics to use to repair cars. She checks the tools back in when the job is done. Last night someone got into the toolroom and stole some expensive tools. The police officer is investigating.

MR. JOHNSON: It seems very strange. The back window is broken. But I can't see where anyone broke into the toolroom.

OFFICER: Who has keys to the toolroom?

MR. JOHNSON: Just Ramona and I. And Ramona gives me her key every night before she leaves.

OFFICER: Ramona, did you give the key to Mr. Johnson last night?

RAMONA: Yes, I handed it to him when he gave me my paycheck, just before I left.

MR. JOHNSON: That's right. Ramona has always been very careful about returning the key.

OFFICER: Well, this looks like someone had a key. Ramona, do you ever leave the key where it could be picked up?

RAMONA: No. I always lock the toolroom if I have to go out, like at lunchtime. And I take the key with me.

MR. JOHNSON: Have you ever let one of the mechanics borrow the key to get a tool while you were at lunch?

RAMONA: Let me think. Yes, I let Joe borrow it one time. But he's my friend, and he brought the key right back.

OFFICER: Right now I don't have any idea who it could be. I'll investigate and let you know what I find out.

(Several days later)

OFFICER: Well, Mr. Johnson, we found the thief and most of the tools.

MR. JOHNSON: Who was it? How did you do it so fast? Where are the tools?

OFFICER: Ramona gave me the clue. I'm sorry, Ramona, but your so-called friend, Joe, was the thief.

RAMONA: How could that be? He gave me back the key.

OFFICER: Sure he did. But before he gave it back, he had a copy of the key made. We were just lucky you remembered giving it to him and told us.

RAMONA: Some friend he was! If Mr. Johnson had thought I had a part in the stealing, I'd have lost my job.

MR. JOHNSON: He just pretended to be your friend to get what he wanted. He quit about a week before the break-in. That must have been right after he got the key made.

RAMONA: I'm glad you'll get back most of the tools, Mr. Johnson. Now I better get back to work.

For more information about this job, see TOOLROOM ATTENDANT in the Dictionary of Job Descriptions in the back of the book.

A • THINGS TO TALK ABOUT

1. What being trustworthy means

2. What being responsible means

3. How someone can pretend to be your friend and really intend to use you for their gain

4. Why employers must safeguard equipment

2. Some words can have endings added. The word without the ending is called the **root word**. Find each root word below. Write it on the line. You may have to add *e* when you take off *ing*. The first one has been done for you.

a. servicing _*service*_____

b. manager _____

c. checks _____

d. worker _____

e. regularly _____

f. training _____

g. customers _____

h. looked _____

3. Match the words that have the same root word. Circle the root words. The first one has been done for you.

(call)ing   servicing

understands   managed

suggestion   friendly

customers   understanding

manager   (call)s

waiting   customer

worker   waits

services   suggests

unfriendly   interesting

interested   work

4. Find four words in the story that have a root word in them. Write the words.

_____

5. Write two good and two bad things about working at a service station.

_____   _____

_____   _____

6. List some of the things a service station worker has to do.

_____

_____

_____

_____

SWEET SUCCESS

STUDY WORDS

awfully
charge
department store
excellent
platform
promote
responsibility
satisfactory
success
warehouse

Tim works in the warehouse of a large department store. Tim likes his job. He has to be very careful. The merchandise must not be scratched or broken. The merchandise is kept in the warehouse until it is needed in the store. Tim helps load things onto the trucks at the loading platform. The trucks take the things to the store. Tim does his job well. He follows directions and tries to do a good job.

Mr. Sims, the warehouse manager, came to visit Tim.

"Hello Tim," said Mr. Sims. "You are doing your job very well."

"Thank you, Mr. Sims," said Tim. "I'm glad my work is satisfactory."

"It is more than satisfactory." said Mr. Sims. "I understand you are the only one on the loading platform who has learned the numbers of each department."

"Well, everything that comes to the warehouse has to go to the right department," said Tim. "It seemed easy to learn that furniture goes to department 15, dishes to department 23, and so on."

"The others haven't learned that," said Mr. Sims. "I'm really proud of you."

Several weeks later Mr. Sims came to the warehouse again.

"Tim, I'd like to promote you to be in charge of the unloading dock," said Mr. Sims.

"I don't know," said Tim. "It seems like an awfully big job for me. I don't know whether or not I can do it."

"I think you can do it," said Mr. Sims. "It won't be much different from what you are already doing."

"It's a lot of responsibility," said Tim. "And I haven't been here as long as some of the others."

"I'd like for you to try the job for a while," said Mr. Sims. "You know all the departments by number. That is what counts in this job. We need someone who can tell the other workers what to do."

"All right, I'll try it," said Tim.

"Good for you," said Mr. Sims. "I'm proud of you. I'm sure you will do the job right. And there will be a nice raise in your next paycheck."

Tim has been in charge of the unloading dock for several months now. He is doing an excellent job. Mr. Sims is well pleased with the way Tim does his work and gets along with the other workers in the warehouse. Tim is happy with the new car he is buying with the extra money from his raise. It has the letters *SS* on the side. Tim says the letters stand for "sweet success."

For more information about this job, see FORKLIFT OPERATOR in the Dictionary of Job Descriptions.

A • THINGS TO TALK ABOUT

1. What a loading platform looks like

2. Why some people are afraid to accept responsibility

3. The similarities and differences of work in a

   • department store warehouse

   • supermarket warehouse

   • variety store warehouse

   • furniture warehouse

4. What things you would be expected to do if you worked in a warehouse

5. Why it is good, sometimes, to do more than is expected of you on the job

6. A G.E.D. (General Equivalency Diploma)

1. What things did Tim do well on his job?

   _____

2. What did Tim learn that the other workers did not?

   _____

3. What promotion was Tim offered?

   _____

4. Why did Tim not want to take the promotion at first?

   _____

C • THINGS TO DO

1. List at least six different departments found in a department store.

   _____

   _____

2. Add *room* to each of these words. The first one has been done for you.

   a. class *classroom*_____ **b.** stock _____

   c. bed _____ **d.** bath _____

3. Write the meaning after each word.

   a. excellent _____

   b. satisfactory _____

   c. promote _____

4. Use each of these words in a sentence.

   a. responsibility_____

   b. success _____

   c. platform _____

A LOOK IN THE MIRROR

STUDY WORDS

applicant
cafeteria
improve
mirror
neatness
necessary
sew
uniform
wrinkled

CHARACTERS

SUE, *a job applicant*
MS. ORTEGA, *the interviewer*

SETTING

An employment office. Sue is applying for a job in the food service department of a hospital.

SUE: Ms. Ortega, do you think you can place me in the cafeteria job?

MS. ORTEGA: Well, Sue, we do have several openings now. But, I'm not sure I can consider you for that kind of work.

SUE: Why not? I'm old enough.

17

MS. ORTEGA: There are other things I have to think about besides your age, Sue. What are some of the things you need to do to be a worker in the food trades?

SUE: Well, it is necessary to be able to get along with people. There are other things too, but I can't remember all of them. But I'm not afraid to work hard. I'll try to do my best.

MS. ORTEGA: There *are* other things that are important, Sue. Go look at yourself in the mirror right now.

(Sue goes to the mirror and looks at herself. Her blouse is wrinkled. It doesn't look ironed. It has a button missing. Her skirt is pinned shut where it should be buttoned. Her hair doesn't look combed.)

SUE: I need to sew a button on my blouse, don't I?

MS. ORTEGA: I think the people in the cafeteria would notice more than that, Sue. Your blouse needs ironing too. Your skirt is pinned and your hair needs combing.

SUE: I'd be wearing a uniform at work, Ms. Ortega. And I'd have a hairnet on my hair.

MS. ORTEGA: Sue, if you come to a job interview wearing a blouse that needs buttons and ironing, maybe you'd forget to keep your uniform neat too. Also, you should be interested in keeping your hair looking nice at all times.

SUE: I'm too tired to fix my hair every night. And sometimes I get in too late to iron everything right.

MS. ORTEGA: Neatness is very important when you are working around people and food. I think you should work on trying to improve your looks before we talk about placing you in a job.

(One week later. Sue is back. This time Ms. Ortega sees a young woman with a neatly ironed dress—no buttons missing—and her hair combed.)

SUE: Ms. Ortega, do you think you have a job for me now?

MS. ORTEGA: Well, Sue. I saw how nice you looked as soon as you walked in. You *have* been trying to improve your appearance.

SUE: Yes, I have. I really want to go to work. I understand now what you were talking about—being neat, I mean.

MS. ORTEGA: I can start you next week, Sue. When you started wanting to be neat, I knew you would soon be ready to go to work. I hope you will keep on trying.

SUE: Oh, yes. I will keep on trying, Ms. Ortega. I feel better about myself when I look nice.

For more information about this job, see CAFETERIA COUNTER SERVER in the Dictionary of Job Descriptions.

A • THINGS TO TALK ABOUT

1. Jobs where neatness might not be so important

2. How some persons might be turned down for a job and not really know why

3. How neatness and cleanliness go together

4. How to get ready for a job interview

1. Where does Sue want to work? _____

2. What was wrong with the way Sue looked?

_____

3. How old do you think Sue is? Why?

_____

4. Why wasn't Sue ready for the interview?

_____

C • THINGS TO DO

1. Use each of these words in a sentence.

   a. improve _____

   b. neatness _____

   c. applicant _____

2. Add *s* to these words to make them mean more than one. The first one has been done for you.

   a. mirror _*mirrors*_____   **b.** uniform _____

   c. worker _____   **d.** friend _____

3. Add *ing* to these words. The first one has been done for you.

   a. comb _*combing*_____   **b.** try _____

   c. need _____   **d.** miss _____

4. Change each of these words to show that the action took place in the past. The first one has been done for you.

   a. comb _*combed*_____   **b.** disappoint _____

   c. iron _____   **d.** place _____

THE DROP-IN

STUDY WORDS

advice
application
dropout
insurance
part-time
permanent
regular
shift
temporary

CHARACTERS

CHIANG, *a high school senior*
DON, *a high school dropout*

SETTING

A movie theater lobby. Chiang and Don are friends. They meet coming out of the movie.

CHIANG: What's happening, Don? What did you think of the movie?

DON: That Jack Nicholson is a great actor. I always like the movies he's in. I wish I had his job.

CHIANG: Better get in line and bring your lunch. And speaking of jobs, have you found one yet?

DON: Nothing permanent. I worked at a few temporary jobs, but they didn't last very long.

CHIANG: What happened to that band you were playing in?

DON: We had several pretty good jobs. But then a couple of the guys got married and moved on to other things. They had to get regular jobs. One or two of the others went away to college. We never see each other anymore.

CHIANG: Can't you get a job in another group?

DON: Guitar players are a dime a dozen. I've called all the groups I know. None of them needs another guitarist. It's a tough situation.

CHIANG: That's too bad. What have you been doing?

DON: Well, I worked a week at a service station. Then I got laid off. The manager said the station's insurance didn't cover anyone under eighteen.

CHIANG: That's too bad. Were you able to find any other jobs?

DON: I got a part-time job sacking groceries. One of the regular sackers was sick.

CHIANG: Couldn't you get a job in a factory?

DON: Most places won't even let you fill out an application unless you have a high school diploma, a G.E.D., or some experience. And even then, you have to start off working the night shift.

CHIANG: That's bad news too. I thought I wanted to drop out of school and go to work, but now I'm not sure.

DON: I wouldn't drop out if I were you. It's no fun looking for a job and getting turned down so often.

CHIANG: Our counselor says if I stay in school this year, he is sure he will be able to place me in some kind of work I like. He wants me to be thinking about the kind of work I want to do. I think I will take his advice and stay in school.

DON: What do you think you want to do?

CHIANG: I've been working in the automotive service shop. I've learned a lot. The teacher says I'll be a good mechanic's helper.

DON: Maybe you can go to work in an auto service center.

CHIANG: I hope so. Well, I promised to be home early. I better get going.

DON: It was good talking to you. Let's get together again soon.

CHIANG: OK. It was good talking to you too. Maybe you'll change your mind and come back to school. *(Leaves)*

DON *(Talking to himself)*: Going back to school might not be such a bad idea at that. I think I'll become a "drop-in."

A • THINGS TO TALK ABOUT

1. The kinds of jobs that are permanent

2. The kinds of jobs that are temporary

3. The difference between full-time and part-time jobs

4. What kinds of jobs might require working shifts

5. Good things and bad things about shift work

6. Good things about full-time work

7. A G.E.D. (General Equivalency Diploma) and how to get one

8. The kinds of jobs that are temporary but full-time

9. The difference between being laid off and being fired

B • QUESTIONS TO ANSWER

1. What is the reason most places will not hire Don?

_____

2. What kind of work has Don been able to get?

_____

3. What did Don tell Chiang about dropping out of school?

_____

4. Where has Chiang been working at school? _____

5. What is Don thinking to himself at the end of the story? _____

C • THINGS TO DO

1. Write the words for these numbers.

   a. 17 _____   **b.** 18 _____

2. Write the meaning of each word.

   a. application _____

   b. permanent _____

   c. temporary _____

   d. shift _____

3. Use each word in a sentence.

   a. regular _____

   b. part-time _____

1. What was Gene's first job? _____

2. What was Gene supposed to be doing on the day described in the story?

   _____

3. What was it Gene did not like about his work?

   _____

4. Was the work too hard? _____

5. Did Mrs. Williams give Gene too much work to do?

   _____

6. Do you think Gene did the right thing when he left his job at the florist shop?

   _____

7. Do you think Gene will stay on his new job? Why?

   _____

C • THINGS TO DO

1. Find each root word. The first one has been done for you.

   a. worried _worry_ _____   **b.** running _____

   c. breaking _____   **d.** supposed _____

   e. stems _____   **f.** finished _____

   g. ordered _____   **h.** scratched _____

   i. scrubbed _____   **j.** learning _____

2. Use each word in a sentence.

   a. responsibility _____

   _____

b. groom _____

_____

c. supervise _____

_____

d. wrap _____

_____

e. florist _____

_____

3. Change these words to show past action. In each word, you will have to change the *y* to *i* and add *ed*. The first one has been done for you.

   a. carry _carried_____ **b.** worry _____

   c. hurry _____ **d.** apply _____

   e. try _____ **f.** dry _____

   g. marry _____ **h.** comply _____

   i. supply _____ **j.** curry _____

4. Sometimes when you add *ing* to a word, you have to add another letter. The letter you add will be the same letter the word ends with. Do the others like the first one.

   a. run _running_____ **b.** cut _____

   c. fit _____ **d.** swim _____

   e. shop _____ **f.** put _____

   g. shun _____ **h.** spin _____

   i. flop _____ **j.** slip _____

5. Add *r* or *er* to these words to make new words. The first one has been done for you.

   a. help _helper_____ **b.** spray _____

   c. own _____ **d.** work _____

   e. plant _____ **f.** dance _____

   g. play _____ **h.** bake _____

TIME AND AGAIN

CHARACTERS

CAROL, *a salesclerk at the candy counter*
KAY, *a salesclerk at the jewelry counter*
MR. BERRY, *the store manager*
Customers in the store

SETTING

A variety store. When Carol goes to lunch, Kay takes care of both counters. When Kay goes to lunch, Carol takes care of both counters. Each girl has a half hour for lunch. Carol always gets back on time. Kay is often late.

KAY (*Coming back from lunch*): Have you been busy? I bought the greatest pair of shoes. Wait until I show them to you.

CAROL: You're late again today, Kay. Mr. Berry looked over this way several times. I don't know whether he was checking on you or

STUDY WORDS

checking
customers
expected
manager
nervous
problems
reminded
salesclerk
stock
straighten
variety
weigh
worthwhile

not. But it seemed to me that he looked angry when he didn't see you.

KAY: Why should he care if I take a few extra minutes once in a while? After I eat lunch, I don't have much time to shop. *(She goes over to her jewelry counter.)*

CAROL *(To herself)*: I don't want to tell Mr. Berry that Kay is late almost every day. But, I feel nervous when he looks at me while I'm doing her work.

KAY *(Calling over from her counter)*: I think we ought to have a longer lunchtime.

CAROL: We'd better get back to work. My counter is all straightened. But I need to weigh some one-pound boxes of peanuts. We have a special price on peanuts this week. I'll be rushed later and won't have time.

KAY *(To herself)*: I should straighten up that earring section. But it hardly seems worthwhile. It just gets messed up again anyway. *(To Carol)* Is my makeup all right? *(She turns and looks in one of the mirrors on her counter.)*

CAROL: Your makeup is all right. Here comes Mr. Berry. You'd better look busy.

(Mr. Berry walks up to Kay's counter. There are several customers looking at jewelry. Kay is putting on lipstick.)

MR. BERRY: Kay, will you come back to my office now, please? *(Steps over to Carol's counter)* Carol, will you please wait on Kay's customers for a few minutes?

CAROL: Of course, Mr. Berry. *(To herself)* She is going to get it now!

(Kay and Mr. Berry walk to the office in the back of the store.)

MR. BERRY: Kay, I have been watching you for several weeks. There are two or three things you need to be reminded of. First, you are late returning from lunch almost every day. Second, your counter should be neater. Third, you spend time putting on makeup and trying on jewelry when there is work to be done. Your under-the-counter stock is not neat. The counter glass is covered with finger marks. You have been here long enough to know what is expected of you. I would like to give you a chance to improve your work habits. Are you willing to try?

KAY: I'm getting tired of that jewelry counter, Mr. Berry. There are too many things to do. Can I work somewhere else in the store?

MR. BERRY: No, Kay. Each counter has its own problems. You know that. It seems you are interested only in your paycheck. You should think about what the customers need.

KAY: Oh, I don't mind working. I like to talk to people. I enjoy helping customers find the things they will buy.

MR. BERRY: That's good. That will help you become a good salesclerk. You just need to do the three things I mentioned before: get back from lunch on time; take care of your counter; and forget about makeup on the job.

KAY: I'll try, Mr. Berry. *(Goes back to work)*

For more information about this job, see SALES-CLERK in the Dictionary of Job Descriptions at the back of this book.

A • THINGS TO TALK ABOUT

1. The importance of being on time—all the time

2. The importance of keeping your work area neat

3. The importance of keeping busy on the job—finding things to do

4. Why changing counters was not the answer to Kay's problem

5. How the duties of a salesclerk might be different at different counters

B • QUESTIONS TO ANSWER

1. Which counter did Kay work? _____

2. Which counter did Carol work? _____

3. What does Kay like to do on her lunchtime? _____

4. Who did Kay's work when she was not there? _____

5. What three things did Mr. Berry say Kay needed to do?

_____

_____

_____

6. Why do you think Kay wanted to work at a different counter?

_____

7. What reason did Mr. Berry give Kay for not moving her to a different counter?

_____

8. Do you think Kay will lose her job or keep it? Why?

_____

C • THINGS TO DO

1. Write the words for these numbers.

   a. 1 _____   **b.** 2 _____

   c. 3 _____   **d.** 4 _____

   e. 5 _____   **f.** 6 _____

2. Each word below is made up of two shorter words. Draw a line between the two words that make up each longer word.

    a. sometimes   **b.** everywhere   **c.** everything

    d. somewhere   **e.** worthwhile

3. Add *ly* to each word below.

    a. late _____   **b.** quick _____

    c. slow _____   **d.** quiet _____

    e. free _____   **f.** loud _____

    g. short _____   **h.** unexpected _____

    i. certain _____   **j.** doubtful _____

4. Find the root word and write it on the line.

    a. lately _____   **b.** problems _____

    c. checking _____   **d.** reminded _____

    e. arranged _____   **f.** mentioned _____

    g. getting _____   **h.** working _____

    i. hardly _____   **j.** doing _____

5. Find the word in the box that means the **opposite** of each word below. Write it next to the word.

seldom	early	unhappy	messy
shorter	dirty	never	play
awake	faster		

    a. always _____   **b.** often _____

    c. happy _____   **d.** late _____

    e. longer _____   **f.** work _____

    g. neat _____   **h.** clean _____

    i. asleep _____   **j.** slower _____

B • QUESTIONS TO ANSWER

1. How old was Mary? _____

2. Where was Mary working? _____

3. What are three things Mary has to do as a table setter?

   _____

   _____

   _____

4. Why do you think Sarah told Mary to fill the sugar bowls? _____

   _____

5. Why did Sarah say "Hush, Mary"? _____

6. Why couldn't Mary say she was sorry? _____

   _____

7. Did Mary get fired or quit her job? _____

C • THINGS TO DO

1. Use each word in a sentence.

   a. bossy _____

   _____

   b. business _____

   _____

   c. argue _____

   _____

   d. apologize _____

   _____

2. Write the word for each number.

a. 14 _____

b. 15 _____

c. 16 _____

d. 17 _____

e. 18 _____

f. 19 _____

g. 13 _____

h. 12 _____

i. 11 _____

j. 20 _____

3. Add *ful* to each to make a new word.

a. help _____

b. play _____

c. care _____

d. truth _____

e. thank _____

f. cheer _____

g. doubt _____

h. spite _____

i. forget _____

j. neglect _____

4. A **contraction** is a word made by putting two words together and leaving out some letters. Write the words from which these contractions are made. The first one has been done for you.

a. I'm _I am_____

b. don't _____

c. she's _____

d. you're _____

e. that's _____

f. what's _____

g. they've _____

h. we'll _____

5. Write the contraction for each pair of words. Remember to use the **apostrophe** (') in place of the letters you leave out. You can find the contractions in the story.

a. will not _won't_____

b. could not _____

c. does not _____

d. I am _____

e. you are _____

f. he is _____

g. do not _____

h. you will _____

i. she will _____

j. he has _____

k. they have _____

l. she is _____

WHO'S THE BOSS?

STUDY WORDS

assistant

list

shelf

stationery

urgent

CHARACTERS

PETE, *the stock clerk and helper*

MS. CLAY, *owner of the store*

MR. WALKER, *Ms. Clay's assistant*

SETTING

A stationery store. Pete is putting goods on a shelf.

MS. CLAY: I have to leave for a while. Mr. Walker, you know what has to be done. Pete, you help Mr. Walker if he needs you. *(Leaves)*

MR. WALKER: Pete, I wish you would get these things for an order. It is marked *urgent.* *(Holds out a list)*

PETE: I have to finish this job.

MR. WALKER: I think that can wait. Why don't you get these things for me first. This is an urgent order.

PETE: I think I ought to finish what I'm doing first. You're not the boss.

MR. WALKER: No, I'm not the boss. But Ms. Clay said you were to work with me if I needed you. You heard her.

PETE: I'll help you later. (*Walks away to the stockroom*)

(*Later that afternoon*)

MS. CLAY: What's the matter, Mr. Walker? You look upset.

MR. WALKER: I need Pete to help me. He won't listen to me. He won't help me.

(*Pete comes out of the stockroom.*)

MS. CLAY: Pete, I told you before I left you were to help Mr. Walker. Why didn't you help him?

PETE: I wanted to finish what I was doing.

MS. CLAY: Mr. Walker has been with me a long time. He knows what things are important. You should have done as he asked.

PETE: He's not my boss. I didn't think I had to do as he said.

MS. CLAY: Pete, it is not your job to decide what is important.

For more information about this job, see SHIPPING AND RECEIVING CLERK in the Dictionary of Job Descriptions.

A • THINGS TO TALK ABOUT

1. Why workers sometimes have to take orders

2. The need to be able to change what you are doing to take care of new situations

3. What to do if different people tell you to do different things

4. Why we have people whose job is to tell others what to do

B • QUESTIONS TO ANSWER

1. Do you think Pete lost his job? Give two reasons.

   _____

2. What does Pete need to learn to do? _____

3. Do we know what kind of work Pete was doing? _____

   Does it make any difference what kind of work he was doing? _____

4. How could Pete have handled this situation differently?

   _____

36

1. Write the meaning of each word.

   a. stationery _____

   b. assistant _____

   c. urgent _____

   d. list _____

   e. shelf _____

2. Make a list of three or four things that you must learn to do on any job.

   _____

   _____

   _____

   _____

3. Add *ing* and *er* to these words.

	ing	**er**
a. employ	_____	_____
b. train	_____	_____
c. buy	_____	_____
d. work	_____	_____
e. listen	_____	_____
f. teach	_____	_____

4. Write the word and the ordinal (the name which shows order) for each number.
   The first one has been done for you.

	name	**ordinal**
a. 1	*one*	*first*
b. 2	_____	_____
c. 3	_____	_____
d. 4	_____	_____
e. 5	_____	_____

ONE CHANCE TOO MANY

STUDY WORDS

ankle

ceramic tile

chance

display

examined

fault

materials

steady

stepladder

Dolores worked afternoons. She worked with Jane. Jane was also doing part-time work. They made up display cards for a ceramic tile company. Sometimes they needed materials from a high shelf. The shelf was higher than they could reach. They used a stepladder to get things from the shelf.

One day, Dolores found she needed some materials off the shelf.

"I need some display cards," said Dolores. "Where is the stepladder?"

"Somebody borrowed it," said Jane.

"I think I can stand on these boxes," said Dolores.

"They don't look very steady to me," said Jane. "I think you should get the stepladder."

Dolores started to get on the boxes.

"They don't look steady to me," said Jane again. "You should be more careful. Mr. Bird told us to use the stepladder."

Dolores stood on the boxes and reached for the cards. She had to reach farther than she expected. The top box turned over. Dolores slipped off the box and fell. She turned her ankle.

"Oh, Dolores!" said Jane. "You have hurt yourself. I'll get Mr. Bird."

Jane went to get Mr. Bird, the manager of the shop. Mr. Bird came hurrying over to Dolores.

"Are you hurt?" asked Mr. Bird.

"I hurt my ankle," said Dolores.

"How did it happen?" asked Mr. Bird.

"I stepped up on those boxes," said Dolores, pointing, "and they fell over."

"Why didn't you use the stepladder?" asked Mr. Bird.

"One of the men borrowed it," said Jane. "I told Dolores to get it back."

"I'm sorry I didn't listen to Jane," said Dolores.

"Wait here," said Mr. Bird. "I'll get someone to take you to the company doctor."

The doctor examined her ankle. "How did you turn your ankle, Dolores?"

"I climbed up on some boxes," said Dolores. "I needed something off a high shelf."

"I am surprised," said the doctor. "Mr. Bird has good safety rules in his shop."

"I know," said Dolores. "It was my fault. I should have used the stepladder. I thought the boxes were safe enough."

"You had better follow the safety rules," said the doctor. "Mr. Bird's shop has a good safety record. He won't keep you if you are careless."

"I know," said Dolores. "But it seemed so much trouble to go after the ladder."

"You must rest this ankle at least three days," said the doctor. "Come back and see me then. And remember the safety rules."

For more information about this job, see SAMPLE WORKER in the Dictionary of Job Descriptions.

A • THINGS TO TALK ABOUT

1. Why companies have safety rules

2. What some common safety signs around a business might be

3. How home and job safety rules might be the same or different

4. What to do if you are hurt on the job

B • QUESTIONS TO ANSWER

1. Was Dolores working full-time or part-time? _____

2. When did Dolores work? _____

3. What did Dolores do that was wrong? _____

4. What should Dolores have done? _____

5. What happened when Dolores fell? _____

C • THINGS TO DO

1. Find each root word. Take off the ending and write the root word on the line. The first one has been done for you.

a. asked *ask*_____   **b.** needed _____

c. climbed _____   **d.** borrowed _____

e. safety _____   **f.** rules _____

g. surprised _____   **h.** decided _____

i. working _____   **j.** boxes _____

k. slipped _____   **l.** tipped _____

2. We must use the word *has* or *have* with some words that show past action. Use *has* and *have* to change each word to show past action. The first one has been done for you.

a. do _*has done*_____   *have done*_____

b. watch _____   _____

c. go _____   _____

d. want _____   _____

e. fall _____   _____

f. bake _____   _____

3. The endings *er* and *est* can make words mean *more* or *most*. *Wetter* means *more wet*, for example. Add *er* and *est* to these words.

                                    er   **est**

a. high   _____   _____

b. slow   _____   _____

c. fast   _____   _____

THE WHISTLER

STUDY WORDS

bothers
fire
seriously
tease
whistle

CHARACTERS

JIM, *a table setter*
MS. LIRA, *manager of the coffee shop*
MR. TAYLOR, *owner of the coffee shop*
TINA, *the cashier*
A customer

SETTING

A hotel coffee shop. Jim has recently gone to work there.

MS. LIRA: How do you like your job, Jim?

JIM: It's OK. It's easy. *(Starts to whistle)*

Ms. Lira: Jim, you can't whistle on the job. It bothers some people—customers and workers.

Jim: I don't see why it should bother them. But I'll stop.

(Ms. Lira goes to the kitchen and comes back. Jim is whistling again.)

Ms. Lira: Jim, you must remember what I said about whistling. It wasn't five minutes ago I told you not to whistle on the job.

Jim *(Stops whistling)*: OK.

(Ms. Lira leaves.)

Jim *(Talking to himself)*: Ms. Lira is just picking on me. She never did like me.

(A week later. Ms. Lira is talking to Mr. Taylor in his office.)

Ms. Lira: Mr. Taylor, I'm sorry to say this, but Jim is just not working out on his job.

Mr. Taylor: What's the matter?

Ms. Lira: He is a good worker and does his work well. But he just doesn't take his job seriously. He is full of fun and likes to tease. When he isn't busy, he goes into the kitchen and dances and sings. He keeps others from doing their work. And he still whistles.

Mr. Taylor: I'm sorry too. Everyone likes him. That's part of his problem.

(Mr. Taylor leaves his office and goes into the dining room. Jim is teasing Tina. He is getting in her way as she tries to make change for a customer.)

Mr. Taylor: Jim, please come into my office. I want to talk to you.

Jim: OK.

Mr. Taylor: I've had a talk with Ms. Lira. She tells me you do your work well but play around too much. Also, you keep other people from doing their work.

Jim: Are you going to fire me? If you are, I'm going to leave right now.

For more information about this job, see TABLE SETTER in the Dictionary of Job Descriptions.

A • THINGS TO TALK ABOUT

1. Things *not* to do on a job

2. Jim's attitude toward his job

3. How people can lose their jobs even when their *work* is good

4. The difference between being fired and quitting

B • QUESTIONS TO ANSWER

1. Where did Jim work?_____

2. What kind of work did Jim do? _____

3. What was Jim doing that Ms. Lira asked him to stop? _____

4. What were some of the other things Jim did that he should not have done?

_____

_____

5. Could Jim do his work well? _____

6. Do you think Jim should be fired or given another chance? Why? _____

_____

C • THINGS TO DO

1. Use each word in a sentence.

a. bothers _____

_____

b. tease _____

_____

c. seriously _____

_____

d. fire _____

_____

e. whistle _____

_____

f. dance _____

_____

g. matter _____

_____

h. kitchen _____

_____

2. Write the number for each word.

    a. six _____   **b.** eleven _____

    c. fifteen _____   **d.** twelve _____

    e. seventeen _____   **f.** four _____

3. Choose the right word. Write it on the line. Look a word up in the dictionary if you are not sure of its meaning or correct use.

    a. The men on the job liked _____ work.
                                their   there

    b. The woman said, "Put the box over _____ ."
                                        their   there

    c. The boss said, "_____ work is not finished."
                     Their   There

4. Find each root word and write it on the line.

    a. getting _____   **b.** doing _____

    c. training _____   **d.** whistling _____

    e. working _____   **f.** going _____

    g. appointment _____   **h.** managing _____

    i. breaking _____   **j.** neglectful _____

5. Change the word to mean more than one. The first one has been done for you.

    a. talk _*talks*_____   **b.** classmate _____

    c. habit _____   **d.** appointment _____

    e. worker _____   **f.** customer _____

    g. act _____   **h.** teacher _____

6. Write one or two sentences to tell how you think the story will end. Answer these questions to help you decide: Do you think Jim will get fired? Will he quit? Will he try to stop bothering other people at work?

_____

_____

_____

_____

_____

TOO MANY EXCUSES

STUDY WORDS

complained

excuses

factory

foolish

ideas

overtime

supervisor

CHARACTERS

BILL, *an unemployed teenager*

DORIS, *a friend*

SETTING

A street corner downtown where Bill hangs out.
Doris is on her lunch break.

DORIS: Hello, Bill. How's your job? Are you still working at the factory?

BILL: No, I'm not working now. I got fired.

DORIS: I'm sorry to hear that. Do you have any ideas about a new job?

45

BILL: No, not right now. I'd like to go back to work at the bakery. I liked that job best.

DORIS: Do you think they would take you back, Bill, after what happened the last time?

BILL: I never did understand why they let me go.

DORIS: I was working at the bakery then. I remember you used to want to leave early every Friday. You wanted to go to your dad's for the weekend.

BILL: I don't think that was the reason. I think it was because I complained about the extra money they took out of my pay.

DORIS: Why did they take extra money out of your pay?

BILL: Because I was late several times.

DORIS: I know that the supervisor was really upset the day you didn't come in at all. It was raining, and you said you didn't want to get wet.

BILL: Well, maybe it wasn't a good reason. I remember she really bawled me out about that.

DORIS: What happened at the factory?

BILL: They asked me to work overtime. I told them I couldn't, because I had a date.

DORIS: Oh, Bill, what a foolish thing to say. They wouldn't have asked you to work overtime unless they needed you.

BILL: I was getting tired of that job anyway. I would rather go back to the bakery.

DORIS: When are you going to check into it?

BILL: I don't want to ask for the job myself. I'll get someone to call for me.

DORIS: If I were you, I would ask for the job back myself. I wouldn't ask someone to do it for me. Well, I have to run now. I don't want to be late getting back to work. Goodbye, Bill.

A • THINGS TO TALK ABOUT

1. The meaning of responsibility

2. How people can show they are responsible

3. Some signs of a mature person

4. The difference between good and poor excuses for being late or missing work

5. Why Bill should not expect to get his job at the bakery back

B • QUESTIONS TO ANSWER

1. Where was Bill's last job? _____

_____

2. Why had Bill been fired from his last job?

_____

3. Write three things Bill did that might have caused him to be fired from the job at the bakery.

_____

_____

4. Why was extra money taken out of Bill's pay?

_____

_____

5. Do you think Bill should call the bakery himself? Why?

_____

_____

6. How did Bill and Doris know each other?

_____

7. Which person seems more mature (grown-up) to you—Bill or Doris? Why?

_____

_____

_____

C • THINGS TO DO

1. Write the meaning of each word.

a. foolish _____

b. complained _____

c. supervisor _____

2. Use each word in a sentence.

a. factory _____

b. excuses _____

c. overtime _____

d. ideas _____

JUST JOKING

STUDY WORDS

cartons

display

item

joke

merchandise

pretending

priced

pricing gun

stockroom

trash

worried

CHARACTERS

HANK, *a sacker and stock clerk*

DAVE, *a sacker and stock clerk*

MS. SCOTT, *assistant store manager*

SETTING

A supermarket stockroom. Hank has played a joke on Dave. Hank hid the pricing gun used to print the price tags for merchandise sold in the store.

HANK: I finished putting up that new display. Ms. Scott told me to come and help you.

DAVE: I can't find the pricing gun.

HANK: Where did you leave it?

DAVE: Right where I always do. Right here on this shelf.

HANK (*Pretending to look for it*): I don't see it anywhere. Are you sure you put it on the shelf?

DAVE: I'm sure. I put it there last night, after I helped unload the truck. I priced some cans and put them on the shelves.

HANK: I went through here several times. I didn't see it. I took some cheese and sandwich meat to be sliced, and I took some meat to the meat counter.

DAVE: (*Looking worried*): I told Ms. Scott I would get this soap marked right away. This is a sale item, and there isn't one left on the shelves in the store.

HANK: (*Grinning to himself*): Maybe it fell off the shelf into the trash or into an empty box.

DAVE: Well, maybe. But wherever it is, I have to find it. I know I left it right here on the shelf where it belongs.

MS. SCOTT (*Coming into the stockroom*): Where are those boxes of soap, Dave? I told you to mark them right away and get them out there on the shelves.

DAVE: I can't find the pricing gun. I was sure I left it right here, but I can't find it.

MS. SCOTT: Well, hurry up! I'm surprised, Dave. You usually get things done when I ask you to. Hank, help Dave find that machine. (*Leaves*)

HANK: Yes, ma'am. Gee, she's upset!

DAVE: So am I!

HANK: I'm sorry, Dave. Here you are. I hid it as a joke.

DAVE: Some joke. What are you trying to do? You want me to get fired?

HANK: I just wanted to have a little fun. I can see I picked the wrong time for that. Here, let me help you. We'll get them done quicker if we work together.

DAVE: You open the cartons and I'll put the prices on the boxes. Then you take a few boxes to the shelves and I'll keep marking prices.

HANK: I'll never pull that trick on you again. Are you going to tell Ms. Scott on me?

DAVE: No. You didn't do it to be mean—but you sure picked a poor time to pull a joke.

HANK: Thanks for being a friend. I wouldn't like to have that on my work record.

For more information about this job, see SUPERMARKET STOCK CLERK in the Dictionary of Job Descriptions.

A • THINGS TO TALK ABOUT

1. The kind of person who would like to work in a supermarket

2. Why many people would not like this kind of work

3. What a work record is and the kinds of things that are on a work record

4. The value of a good work record

5. Why Hank's joke was not so funny

1. What do stock clerks do? _____

_____

2. What is a sale item? _____

3. What did Hank do that he should not have done?

_____

4. Do you think Dave was angry with Hank? Give a reason for your answer. _____

_____

5. Do you think Dave should have told Ms. Scott what Hank did? Why? _____

_____

C • THINGS TO DO

1. Some words are made to mean more than one by changing their spelling. Make each word below mean more than one. Change the *f* to *v* and add *es*. The first one has been done for you.

   a. shelf *shelves* _____   **b.** leaf _____

   c. half _____   **d.** loaf _____

2. Find each root word and write it on the line.

   a. worker _____   **b.** displays _____

   c. customers _____   **d.** decided _____

   e. asked _____   **f.** boxes _____

   g. grinning _____   **h.** quicker _____

3. Use each word in a sentence.

   a. merchandise _____

   b. trash _____

TIME FOR A CHANGE

STUDY WORDS

courteous

mistakes

nervous

upset

waitress

Nell worked as a waitress at the counter in a lunchroom. The lunchroom was in a big store downtown. Nell had been working there six months. She was a good worker. She was neat and clean. She was courteous. She did all the things she was supposed to do.

But Nell was a very nervous person. When she got upset, her hands shook. She forgot some of her orders. Sometimes she mixed up her orders.

Nell had a boyfriend named Charles. Charles worked downtown too. He liked to eat at the counter in the lunchroom so he could see Nell. Nell got upset when Charles came to

51

eat while she was working. Charles didn't do anything to upset Nell. But she got nervous anyway.

Nell's employer was Mrs. Brown. Mrs. Brown noticed that Nell got nervous when Charles ate at the lunchroom. Mrs. Brown spoke to Charles about Nell.

"Charles," said Mrs. Brown, "it bothers Nell to have you come to eat while she is working."

"I don't bother her," said Charles. "And I don't keep her from working."

"You don't do anything to bother her," said Mrs. Brown, "but she gets very nervous while you are here."

"Well, that's a fine thing!" said Charles. "Everybody in the country can eat here but me." Charles was angry.

"If it means Nell will lose her job, will you still come here?" asked Mrs. Brown.

"It doesn't make any sense to me," said Charles, "but if it will make things better for Nell. I will stay away."

"Thank you, Charles," said Mrs. Brown. "I think Nell will thank you too."

Charles stayed away for awhile. Nell did not get upset. She did her work very well.

But Charles did not stay away for long. He came back to eat in the lunchroom. Again Nell got nervous. She made mistakes in her work. She forgot some orders. She dropped a tray. Another day she broke some dishes.

Mrs. Brown owned a lunchroom in another store. Mrs. Brown sent Nell to work there. This job was not downtown. Charles could not go there to eat his lunch.

Nell likes her new job. She is doing very well. She does not get nervous. She does not forget things. She hasn't broken any dishes. The manager likes Nell and the way she does things.

Charles and Nell are still dating. Sometimes Charles tells Nell he wishes she still worked downtown. He misses seeing her at lunchtime. Nell doesn't say anything. She knows it is better for her to be working where she is.

For more information about this job, see WAITER/WAITRESS and LUNCHROOM COUNTER ATTENDANT in the Dictionary of Job Descriptions.

A • THINGS TO TALK ABOUT

1. The importance of doing what is best for others

2. Ways to show respect for the rights of others

3. The duties of a waiter or waitress

4. The kind of person that would make a good waiter or waitress

5. The reason Nell herself did not tell Charles that he made her nervous

6. Why Charles got angry at Mrs. Brown

7. Things you might like about being a waiter or waitress

8. Things you might not like about being a waiter or waitress

1. Why did Mrs. Brown speak to Charles about Nell?

_____

2. How long had Nell been working at the lunchroom?

_____

3. How did Nell act when Charles came to eat where she worked? _____

4. Do you think everyone would be as easily upset as Nell? _____

5. Do you think Charles really understood Nell's problem?

_____

6. How did changing jobs help Nell? _____

_____

C • THINGS TO DO

1. Rewrite each sentence. Leave out the underlined word. Put the meaning of the underlined word in its place. Use the Glossary if you need help.

   a. Nell was <u>courteous</u>.

   _____

   b. Are you <u>upset</u>?

   _____

   c. She left a tip for the <u>waitress</u>.

   _____

2. Write the word for each number.

   a. 19 _____   b. 6 _____

   c. 20 _____   d. 15 _____

53

3. Write the names of the months of the year and their abbreviations (shortened spellings). Begin with the first month.

1. _____

2. _____

3. _____

4. _____

5. _____

6. _____

7. _____

8. _____

9. _____

10. _____

11. _____

12. _____

4. Draw a line between the two words that make up each word.

a. lunchtime   **b.** everyone   **c.** lunchroom

d. downtown   **e.** upset   **f.** everybody

g. boyfriend   **h.** anything   **i.** sometimes

5. Choose the right word. Write it on the line.

a. Will you still come _____ ?
         here   hear

b. Chester works downtown _____ .
         to   too

c. Nell and _____ have been going steady.
         me   I

d. Nell made _____ mistakes yesterday.
         to   two

e. Ms. Jones wanted _____ to move.
         she   her

f. She gave _____ her answer.
         him   he

MORE FUN THAN WORK

George went to work as a dishwasher. The work was not too hard. George did his work well.

All George had to do was put dirty dishes, glasses, and silverware in the racks. A conveyor took them through the dishwasher. George had to press one button for water. He had to press another button for steam.

Tom worked with George. Tom was a dishwasher too. Tom took the clean dishes off the conveyor.

Tom and George liked working together. Sometimes there were no dirty dishes to wash. They had time to talk.

One day when George was not busy, he popped Tom with a towel.

"Ouch!" said Tom. "Quit that."

George just grinned and popped him again.

This time their boss, Ms. Jackson, saw George.

"George," said Ms. Jackson, "that isn't what towels are for!"

"I know, Ms. Jackson. I'm sorry," said George.

"It seems you are always being sorry for something," said Ms. Jackson. "Yesterday you were sorry you argued with the elevator operator. The day before that you were sorry you cursed one of the cooks."

"I know, Ms. Jackson," said George. "It seems I'm always getting into trouble. But I don't mean to."

"You will have to learn to discipline yourself," said Ms. Jackson. "This is a place to work, not play. If it were just once in a while, I wouldn't say anything. But you do something wrong every day."

"I'll try to do better," said George.

For a day or two, George did do better. But his good behavior didn't last. One day he playfully threw a biscuit at the elevator operator. Several times he went upstairs to the laundry and stayed a long time. No one knew where he was.

Ms. Jackson had to talk to George again. "I'm sorry, George, but if you don't do better, I'll have to let you go."

"Gee, Ms. Jackson, I don't want to get fired," said George. "Give me another chance."

"You've had all the chances I can give you," said Ms. Jackson. "Maybe getting fired is what you need."

For more information about this job, see DISH-WASHER in the Dictionary of Job Descriptions.

A • THINGS TO TALK ABOUT

1. What we mean by "knowing when to be serious"

2. Why saying you're sorry isn't always enough

3. What *not* to do when you're not busy on the job

4. Some things you *can* do when not busy on the job

5. What self-discipline is and how to develop it

6. How to adjust your behavior to your job

B • QUESTIONS TO ANSWER

1. What kind of job did George have? _____

2. List three things George did that he should not have done.

_____

_____

3. Did George do his work well? _____ In what paragraph did you find the answer?

_____

4. Did George do better after Ms. Jackson talked to him? _____

5. What does George need to learn? _____

_____

C • THINGS TO DO

1. Write the meaning of each word.

   a. conveyor _____

   b. discipline _____

2. Add *er* and *est* to each word. Remember to change *y* to *i*.

	er	**est**
a. long	*longer*	*longest*
b. smart		
c. busy		
d. hard		
e. sorry		

3. Sometimes we use *more* and *most* instead of *er* and *est*. Put *more* and *most* in front of each word.

	more		**most**	
a.	*more*	responsible	*most*	responsible
b.		comfortable		comfortable
c.		wasteful		wasteful

57

SLOW BUT SURE

STUDY WORDS

breaktime
complaints
delivers
department
explained
messenger
research
schedule
sort
visit

CHARACTERS

AMY, *a messenger*
MS. WILLIAMS, *office manager*

SETTING

The office manager's office in a large company. Amy is doing temporary work. She helps sort mail and delivers it to different departments in the company. Ms. Williams stopped Amy during her morning delivery. Ms. Williams told Amy to come to her office when she was through.

AMY: I'm back, Ms. Williams. You said you wanted to talk to me.

MS. WILLIAMS: That's right. But you said you'd

be through in fifteen minutes. That was half an hour ago.

AMY: Yeah. I got to talking to Jan in the research department. We're going to the show together tonight.

MS. WILLIAMS: You have a schedule to follow, Amy. Now you are behind.

AMY: I'll hurry. Maybe I can catch up.

MS. WILLIAMS: That is what I want to talk to you about. I've had complaints about you being late in getting to several departments.

AMY: I always get through before the day is over.

MS. WILLIAMS: Yes, but your schedule shows you should be through an hour before you leave. That gives you time to sort the late mail delivery for the next day.

AMY: I can sort that mail the next morning.

MS. WILLIAMS: When you started working here, we explained your schedule and why it is important to do things according to the schedule. Mail delivery is very important to every department so they can get their work done. You have to keep your schedule so they can keep theirs. You will have to do your visiting during your breaktime.

AMY: I guess I forgot. I'm sorry. Everyone is so friendly. I guess I just visit too much along the way.

MS. WILLIAMS: You are a good worker. You are friendly and well liked. I'd like to keep you on after the regular mail messenger gets back.

AMY: I'd like to stay. I like working here. I'll get back on schedule and stay there.

MS. WILLIAMS: Thank you, Amy. Now let's both get back to work.

For more information about this job, see OFFICE MESSENGER in the Dictionary of Job Descriptions.

A • THINGS TO TALK ABOUT

1. What "a day's work for a day's pay" means

2. Why schedules are important

3. How we live with schedules all through our lives

4. The importance of following directions

5. How the attitude of supervisors can make work pleasant or unpleasant

6. How your attitude toward the company you work for can make a difference in your work

7. How schedules change with vacations, school, work, and weekends

8. The importance of putting your work first while you are on the job

1. What does Amy do on her job? _____

_____

2. Why does Amy have to follow a schedule?

_____

3. Was Ms. Williams angry with Amy? _____

4. Why did Ms. Williams explain to Amy what she was doing wrong?

_____

5. When could Amy talk to her friends and not get behind on her schedule?

_____

C • THINGS TO DO

1. Write your daily schedule.

Morning	Afternoon	Evening

2. Change each word to show that the action took place in the past.

a. work _____

b. decide _____

c. help _____

d. push _____

e. explain _____

f. talk _____

g. finish _____

h. sort _____

3. Change the spelling of each word to show that the action took place in the past. Use a dictionary if you need help.

a. do _____

b. leave _____

c. have _____

d. forget _____

e. say _____

f. think _____

g. go _____

h. buy _____

i. cry _____

j. drive _____

k. dig _____

l. dive _____

4. Write the number of minutes for each time.

a. a half hour _____

b. a quarter hour _____

c. one hour _____

d. an hour and a half _____

e. two hours _____

f. two and a quarter hours _____

5. Find each root word. Write it on the line.

a. explained _____

b. complaints _____

c. friendly _____

d. being _____

e. stopped _____

f. delivery _____

g. delivering _____

h. worker _____

i. working _____

j. liked _____

READING IS THE KEY

STUDY WORDS

agency
ashamed
employment counselor
empty
experience
housekeeper
list
openings
scrape
venetian blinds

CHARACTERS

LOUISE, *a housekeeper*
MR. GONZALES, *an employment counselor*

SETTING

An employment agency. Louise wants to go to work. She is talking to the employment counselor.

LOUISE: Do you have any openings for someone with no experience?

MR. GONZALES: Yes, we have a job at a home for the elderly. Do you think you would like that?

LOUISE: What would I have to do?

MR. GONZALES: The work would not be hard,

but there would be many things to do. You would set the tables for meals. After the meals, you would clear the tables. You would scrape the dishes and put them in the dishwasher.

LOUISE: What else would I do?

MR. GONZALES: You would have to empty the wastebaskets and dust the furniture. Then you would have to clean the bathrooms.

LOUISE: I guess I could do that.

MR. GONZALES: Dusting the venetian blinds and washing windows would need to be done about once a week. There might be a few other things to do, but not many. I think you will be able to do it.

LOUISE: It doesn't sound too hard. I would like to try it. How many hours will I work?

MR. GONZALES: You will work from seven in the morning until three in the afternoon. You can start tomorrow. You can go this afternoon to see Ms. Thomas, the manager.

(Two weeks later, at the employment agency)

LOUISE: Hello, Mr. Gonzales. I'm back. I got fired.

MR. GONZALES: Yes, I know. Ms. Thomas called me. I was surprised. She said you were not a good worker. She said you just stood around waiting for her to tell you what to do.

LOUISE: I think she got mad because I didn't dust the venetian blinds.

MR. GONZALES: Why didn't you dust them?

LOUISE: She went out and left a list of things for me to do. And, um, I guess I couldn't read it.

MR. GONZALES: I see, Why didn't you tell Ms. Thomas?

LOUISE: I was ashamed to let Ms. Thomas know I can't read so good.

MR. GONZALES: She would have understood. And there is no reason for you to be ashamed. Would you like to improve your reading?

LOUISE: Yes. Not being able to read is a real drag.

MR. GONZALES: I know just where you need to go. One of the businesses we deal with has a training program. You can work and go to class too. You will be paid to go to class.

LOUISE: Really? That sounds great. I think I'd like to work at a place where I can get help.

For more information about this job, see CLEANER in the Dictionary of Job Descriptions.

A • THINGS TO TALK ABOUT

1. Some of the things you have to do on different jobs

2. Kinds of jobs where you would be expected to keep yourself busy

3. Places that would offer jobs similar to the one in this situation

4. Kinds of jobs where you might have only one thing to do

5. Some things that might help you decide what kind of job you might like to have

B • QUESTIONS TO ANSWER

1. Write six things Louise was expected to do.

_____

_____

_____

2. How many hours a day did Louise work?

_____

3. Why didn't the list of things help Louise?

_____

4. Why did Louise let herself be fired?

_____

5. How could Louise have kept from being fired?

_____

C • THINGS TO DO

1. Write the meaning of each word.

   a. list _____

   b. scrape _____

   c. empty _____

   d. openings _____

2. Use each word in a sentence.

   a. ashamed _____

   b. agency _____

   c. experience _____

THE LAST DETAIL

STUDY WORDS

attention

attitude

careless

complaint

manager

realize

Beverly worked in the school cafeteria. She was a helper at the serving counter. She took trays of food from the refrigerator to the counter. The other workers put the food in the counter as it was needed. Beverly took the empty trays back to the kitchen.

Beverly liked her job very much. She liked the people she worked with. She liked Ms. Smith, the manager.

One day Ms. Smith's supervisor, Mr. Chapa, visited the kitchen. Beverly saw Ms. Smith and Mr. Chapa talking. Once they looked at her. She wished she could hear what they were saying.

If she had been able to hear them, she would not have been happy.

"Ms. Smith, I need to talk to you about Beverly," said Mr. Chapa.

"What's the matter, Mr. Chapa?" asked Ms. Smith. "Beverly is doing very well with her job."

"Oh, I have no complaint about Beverly's work," said Mr. Chapa. "But Beverly is careless about keeping her hands and fingernails clean and looking right. She doesn't seem to understand how important it is to have clean hands and nails in this job."

"I'm sorry Beverly has been so careless," said Ms. Smith. "I'll talk to her before she leaves today."

Ms. Smith took Beverly aside later that day. "I want to talk to you, Beverly," said Ms. Smith. "Do you like your work in the cafeteria?"

"Oh, yes, Ms. Smith, I like it very much," said Beverly.

"Do you remember the things we talked about before you started work?" asked Ms. Smith. "About jobs, I mean."

"Do you mean all the things about getting along with others, following directions, being on time, and things like that?" asked Beverly.

"Yes, Beverly," said Ms. Smith. "That is what I mean. Can you think of another important thing to remember? One that is most important for people working with food."

"Being neat and clean," said Beverly. "Uh oh, now I think I know why you wanted to talk to me. I saw Mr. Chapa talking to you. I wondered if you were talking about me."

"Do you think you know what he said to me?" asked Ms. Smith.

"Yes, I think I know," said Beverly. "Was it about keeping my hands and fingernails clean?"

"You are right," said Ms. Smith.

"I didn't mean to forget," said Beverly. "I have been working in the yard after work. I have been planting flowers and pulling weeds. I get my hands dirty, and my nail polish gets chipped too. I guess I should wear gloves to work in the yard."

Beverly looked at her hands and showed them to Ms. Smith.

"They do need fixing up, don't they?" said Beverly.

"Yes, they do," said Ms. Smith.

"I'll clean them well before I come in tomorrow," said Beverly. "Tonight I'll file my nails and put fresh polish on them. I'll remember every day, Ms. Smith."

"I'm glad you realize your mistake, Beverly," said Ms. Smith. "You are a good worker. I want you to keep working for me."

"I'm sorry Mr. Chapa had to talk to you about me," said Beverly. "I should have paid more attention to my hands."

"Your attitude is very good, Beverly," said Ms. Smith. "You will be ready for a raise in pay soon."

For more information about this job, see CAFE-TERIA COUNTER SERVER in the Dictionary of Job Descriptions.

A • THINGS TO TALK ABOUT

1. Why cleanliness is so important around food

2. How neatness and cleanliness go together

3. Should a health card be required for people who work around food

4. The importance of good attitudes

5. The importance of being able to take criticism without getting angry or upset

6. The importance of listening and asking for things to be made clear

B • QUESTIONS TO ANSWER

1. Where is Beverly working? _____

2. What does Beverly do? _____

   _____

3. What did Mr. Chapa say about Beverly?

   _____

4. Did Ms. Smith have to tell Beverly what she had done wrong? _____

5. What did Beverly decide to do? _____

6. Did Beverly lose her job? Why? _____

   _____

C • THINGS TO DO

1. Write the meaning of each word.

   a. realize _____

   b. attention _____

   c. attitude _____

   d. careless _____

2. Add *ing* to each word.

   a. play _____   b. work _____

c. plant _____   **d.** keep_____

e. follow _____   **f.** be _____

3. Draw lines to match the words that mean the **opposite**.

clean	lead
follow	forget
late	careful
remember	early
careless	dirty
morning	play
work	evening

4. Adding *un* to a word makes the word mean *not*. For example, *untied* means *not tied*. Put *un* in front of each word to change the meaning. The first one is done for you.

a. folded *unfolded* _____   **b.** important_____

c. happy _____   **d.** clean _____

e. finished _____   **f.** covered _____

5. Find the root word. Write it on the line.

a. likes_____   **b.** following _____

c. napkins _____   **d.** meant _____

e. complaint_____   **f.** pulling _____

g. looking _____   **h.** chipped_____

i. hands _____   **j.** leaves _____

k. sitting _____   **l.** served _____

6. Write the days of the week that Beverly works. Write the abbreviations for those words.

_____

_____

_____

_____

_____

finish (fin-ish)—complete, bring to end

fire (fire)—let go, dismiss, or discharge (an employee)

florist (flor-ist)—a person who raises and/or sells flowers

foolish (fool-ish)—silly, not wise or smart

funeral spray (fu-ner-al spray)—flowers arranged in a special way for a funeral

groom (groom)—take care of the looks of, make neat and tidy

housekeeper (house-keep-er)—a person who cleans and cares for a building

ideas (i-de-as)—thoughts

improve (im-prove)—become better; make better

insurance (in-sur-ance)—an agreement to pay someone for a loss

interesting (in-ter-est-ing)—holding the attention

investigate (in-ves-ti-gate)—examine closely, search into

item (i-tem)—separate thing or article

joke (joke)—something said or done to make people laugh; trick played on someone

laundry (laun-dry)—a room or building where clothes are cleaned; dirty clothes or linens

list (list)—a paper with things to do or remember written on it

manager (man-ag-er)—person in charge, boss

materials (ma-ter-i-als)—supplies needed to make something

mechanic (me-chan-ic)—a person who makes repairs

merchandise (mer-chan-dise)—things bought and sold

messenger (mes-sen-ger)—person who carries mail to different people

mirror (mir-ror)—a glass in which you can see yourself

mistakes (mis-takes)—things done wrong

neatness (neat-ness)—being clean and in order

necessary (nec-es-sar-y)—required, must be had or done

nervous (ner-vous)—easily excited or upset

openings (o-pen-ings)—jobs for which people are needed

operate (op-er-ate)—to make run or to make work

overtime (o-ver-time)—hours of work past regular hours

part-time (part-time)—a few hours a day or week

payday (pay-day)— the day wages are given for work done

permanent (per-ma-nent)—lasting, not for a short time.

permits (per-mits)—written passes letting people go somewhere or do something

planters (plant-ers)—fancy containers for plants

platform (plat-form)—a raised level surface

pretend (pre-tend, pre-tend-ing)—to make believe; trying to make something seem true

priced (priced)—put price tags on

pricing gun (pric-ing gun)—a small machine that prints prices

problems (prob-lems)—things to be worked out

program (pro-gram)—a plan of what is to be done

projector (pro-jec-tor)—a machine for showing motion pictures or slides

promote (pro-mote)—raise in rank or importance

quit (quit)—leave, stop working at a place

racks (racks)—frames with shelves to keep things on

raise (raise)—an increase in pay

realize (re-a-lize)—to understand clearly

regular (reg-u-lar, reg-u-lar-ly)—steady, coming again and again at the same time

reminded (re-mind-ed)—helped to remember

repair (re-pair)—put in good condition again

report (re-port)—tell on

research (re-search)—a careful hunting for facts or truth

responsibility (re-spon-si-bil-i-ty)—doing what one should do

salesclerk (sales-clerk)—a person whose job is selling in a store

satisfactory (sat-is-fac-to-ry)—good enough, all right

schedule (sched-ule)—a list of times by which certain things must be done

scrape (scrape)—remove

scratched (scratched)—cut a little with something sharp

seriously (ser-i-ous-ly)—not fooling or joking; with careful thought

sew (sew)—work with a needle and thread, fasten with stitches

shelf (shelf)—a flat piece of wood or metal to put things on

shift (shift)—the time one must work

sort (sort)—separate from others; arrange by kinds

stacks (stacks)—piles of things

stationery (sta-tion-er-y)—paper and other supplies for writing or typing

steady (stead-y)—stable

steam (steam)—the gas from boiling water

stems (stems)—the parts of a flower that hold them up

stepladder (step-lad-der)—ladder with flat steps for climbing up and down

stock (stock)—things for use or sale

stockroom (stock-room)—place where supplies are kept until needed

straighten (straight-en)—put in proper order or condition

success (suc-cess)—the gaining of what one wants

supervise (su-per-vise)—look after and direct work of workers

supervisor (su-per-vis-or)—a person who directs the work of others

tease (tease)—bother

temporary (tem-po-rar-y)—lasting for a short time only

thief (thief)—a person who steals

toolroom (tool-room)—a room where tools are kept when not in use

training (train-ing)—working in a job while learning about it

trash (trash)—worthless stuff

tray (tray)—a flat holder with a rim for carrying dishes, glasses, and other things

uniform (u-ni-form)—clothes like everyone else's that must be worn when working

upset (up-set)—bothered

urgent (ur-gent)—needing attention quickly

variety (va-ri-e-ty)—a number of different kinds of things

vases (vas-es)—holders for flowers

venetian blinds (ve-ne-tian blinds)—a special kind of window shade made of slats

visit (vis-it)—go to see and talk to

waitress (wait-ress)—a woman who waits on customers at a table or counter in an eating place

warehouse (ware-house)—a place where goods are kept

weigh (weigh)—to find out how heavy a thing is

whistle (whis-tle)—a clear sound made by blowing through the lips or teeth

worried (wor-ried)—feeling anxious or uneasy, bothered

worthwhile (worth-while)—having real value

wrap (wrap)—cover by folding paper around

wrinkled (wrin-kled)—not ironed, having many creases or folds

wrong (wrong)—not right; not good

DICTIONARY OF JOB DESCRIPTIONS

The job descriptions in this dictionary are from the *Dictionary of Occupational Titles*, Fourth Edition (U.S. Department of Labor, 1977). Check with your public library if you need more information.

CAFETERIA COUNTER SERVER

Serves food from counters and steamtables to cafeteria patrons: Serves salads, vegetables, meat, breads, and cocktails; ladles soups and sauces; portions desserts; and fills beverage cups and glasses as indicated by customer. Adds relishes and garnishes according to instructions from counter supervisor. Scrubs and polishes counters, steamtables, and other equipment. May replenish foods at serving stations. May brew coffee and tea. May carve meat. May accept payment for food, using cash register or adding machine to total check. May prepare and serve salads.

CLEANER

Maintains premises of commercial, institutional, or industrial establishments, office buildings, hotels and motels, apartment houses, retirement homes, nursing homes, hospitals, schools, or similar establishments in clean and orderly condition, performing the following duties: Cleans rooms, hallways, lobbies, lounges, restrooms, corridors, elevators, stairways, and locker rooms and other areas. Sweeps, scrubs, waxes, and polishes floors, using brooms and mops and powered scrubbing and waxing machines. Cleans rugs, carpets, upholstered furniture, and draperies, using vacuum cleaner. Dusts furniture and equipment. Polishes metalwork, such as fixtures and fittings, and marble surfaces. Washes walls, ceiling, and woodwork. Washes windows, door panels, and sills. Empties wastebaskets, and empties and cleans ashtrays. Transports trash and waste to disposal area. Replenishes supplies. Replaces light bulbs.

DISHWASHER

Performs any combination of the following duties to maintain kitchen work areas and restaurant equipment and utensils in clean and orderly condition: Sweeps and mops floors. Washes worktables, walls, refrigerators, and meat blocks. Sorts and removes trash and garbage and places it in designated containers. Steam-cleans or hoses-out garbage cans. Sorts bottles, and breaks disposable ones in bottle crushing machine. Washes pots, pans, and trays by hand. Scrapes food from dirty dishes and washes them by hand or places them in racks or on conveyor or dishwashing machine. Polishes silver, using burnishing-machine tumbler, chemical dip, buffing wheel, and hand cloth. Holds inverted glasses over revolving brushes to clean inside surfaces. Transfers supplies and equipment between storage and work areas by hand or by use of hand truck. Sets up banquet tables. Washes and peels vegetables, using knife or peeling machine.

FLORAL ARRANGER

Under the direction of floral designer, fashions live, cut, dried, and artificial floral and foliar arrangements for events, such as holidays, anniversaries, weddings, balls, and funerals: Confers with client regarding price and type of arrangement desired. Plans arrangement according to client's requirements and costs, utilizing knowledge of design and foliage necessary for arrangement. Trims material and arranges bouquets, sprays, wreaths, dish gardens, terrariums, and other items, using wire, pins, floral tape, foam, trimmers, cutters, shapers, and other materials and tools. May decorate buildings, halls, churches, or other facilities where events are planned. May conduct classes or demonstrations. May instruct and direct workers.

FORKLIFT OPERATOR

Drives gasoline-, liquified gas-, or electric-powered industrial truck equipped with lifting devices, such as forklift, boom, scoop, lift beam and swivel-hook, fork-grapple, clamps, elevating platform, or trailer hitch, to push, pull, lift, stack, tier, or move products, equipment, or materials in warehouse, storage yard, or factory: Moves levers and presses pedals to drive truck and control movement of lifting apparatus. Positions forks, lifting platform, or other lifting device under, over, or around loaded pallets, skids, boxes, products, or materials, or hooks tow trucks to trailer hitch, and transports load to designated area. Unloads and stacks material by raising and lowering materials as needed. May weigh materials or products and record weight on tags, labels, or production schedules. May load or unload materials onto or off pallets, skids, or lifting devices. May lubricate truck, recharge batteries, fill fuel tank, or replace liquified-gas tank.

LUNCHROOM COUNTER ATTENDANT

Serves food to diners seated at the counter: Calls orders to kitchen and picks up and serves order when ready. Accepts payment or makes itemized check for service. May prepare sandwiches, salads, and other short-order items. May perform other duties, such as cleaning counters, washing dishes, and selling cigars and cigarettes.

OFFICE MESSENGER

Performs any combination of the following duties in business office of commercial or industrial establishment: Furnishes workers with clerical supplies. Opens, sorts, and distributes incoming mail, and collects, seals, and stamps outgoing mail. Delivers oral or written messages. Collects and distributes paperwork, such as records or timecards, from one department to another. Marks, tabulates, and files articles and records. May use office equipment, such as envelope-sealing machine, letter opener, record shaver, stamping machine, and transcribing machine. May deliver items to other business establishments. May specialize in delivering mail, messages, documents, and packages between departments of establishment.

PROJECTIONIST

Sets up and operates motion picture projection and sound-reproducing equipment to produce coordinated effects on screen: Inserts film into top magazine reel of projector. Threads film through picture aperture of projector, around pressure rollers, sprocket wheels, and sound drum or magnetic sound pickup on film, and onto spool that automatically takes up slack. Regulates projection light and adjusts sound-reproducing equipment. Monitors operation and transfers operation from one machine to another without interrupting the flow of action on screen. Rewinds broken end of film onto reels by hand to minimize loss of time. Inspects and rewinds projected films for another showing. Repairs faulty sections of film. Operates stereopticon (magic lantern) or other special-effects equipment to project picture slides on screen. Cleans lenses, oils equipment, and makes minor repairs and adjustments.

SALESCLERK

Sells merchandise to individuals in store and showroom, utilizing knowledge of products sold: Greets customer on sales floor and ascertains make, type, and quality of merchandise desired. Displays merchandise, suggests selections that meet customer's needs, and emphasizes selling points of article, such as quality and utility. Prepares sales slip or sales contract. Receives payment or obtains credit authorization. Places new merchandise on display. May wrap merchandise for customer. May take inventory of stock. May requisition merchandise from stockroom.

SAMPLE WORKER

Prepares articles for use as display samples, performing any combination of following duties: Assembles articles into sets. Pins or glues identification tickets or labels to articles. Wraps paper bands around article, securing ends of band with glue, inserts articles into plastic or cellophane bags, or glues articles to cards. Arranges articles in boxes in attractive display and stores samples according to style, size, and color. Fills orders following order ticket. Records number of articles received, sample sets prepared, and samples shipped. Inventories samples in stock and requisitions replacement articles. May tend machine to print identification tickets or labels.

SERVICE STATION ATTENDANT

Services automobiles, buses, trucks, and other automotive vehicles with fuel, lubricant, and accessories: Fills fuel tank of vehicles with gasoline or diesel fuel to level specified by customer. Observes level of oil crankcase and amount of water in radiator, and adds required amounts of oil and water. Adds necessary amount of water to battery, and washes windshield of vehicle. Lubricates vehicle and changes motor oil. Replaces accessories such as oil filter, air filter, windshield wiper blades, and fan belt. Installs antifreeze and changes spark plugs. Repairs or replaces tires. Replaces lights, and washes and waxes vehicle. Collects cash from customer for purchases and makes change or charges purchases, using customer charge plate. May adjust brakes. May sell batteries and automobile accessories usually found in service stations. May assist in arranging displays, taking inventories, and making daily reports.

SHIPPING AND RECEIVING CLERK

Verifies and keeps records on incoming and outgoing shipments and prepares items for shipment: Compares identifying information and counts, weighs, or measures items of incoming and outgoing shipments to verify against bills of lading, invoices, orders, or other records. Determines method of shipment, utilizing knowledge of shipping procedures, routes, and rates. Assembles wooden or cardboard containers or selects preassembled containers. Inserts items into containers, using spacers, fillers, and protective padding. Nails covers on wooden crates and binds containers with metal tape, using strapping machine. Stamps, stencils, or glues identifying information and shipping instructions onto crates or containers. Posts weights and shipping charges and affixes postage. Unpacks and examines incoming shipments, rejects damaged items, records shortages, and corresponds with shipper to rectify damages and shortages. Routes items to departments. May operate tier-lift truck or use hand truck to move, convey, or hoist shipments from shipping-and-receiving platform to storage or work area. May direct others in preparing outgoing and receiving incoming shipments. May perform only shipping and receiving activities.

SUPERMARKET STOCK CLERK

Performs any combination of following duties in self-service store: Marks order form to order merchandise based on available space, merchandise on hand, customer demand, or advertised specials. Periodically counts merchandise to take inventory or examines shelves to identify which items need to be reordered or replenished. Unpacks cartons and crates of merchandise, checking invoice against items received. Stamps or attaches prices on merchandise or changes price tags, referring to pricelist. Stocks shelves with new or transferred merchandise. Sets up advertising signs and displays merchandise on shelves, counters, or tables to attract customer and promote sales. Cleans display cases, shelves, and aisles. May itemize and total customer's selection at checkout counter, using cash register, and make change or charge purchases. May pack customer's purchase in bags or cartons. May carry packages to customer's automobile.

TABLE SETTER

Performs any combination of the following duties to facilitate food service: Carries dirty dishes from dining room to kitchen. Replaces soiled table linens and sets tables with silverware and glassware. Replenishes supply of clean linens, silverware, glassware, and dishes in dining room. Supplies service bar with food, such as soups, salads, and desserts. Serves ice water and butter to patrons. Cleans and polishes glass shelves and doors of service bars and equipment, such as coffee urns and cream and milk dispensers. Runs errands and delivers food orders to offices. May transfer food and dishes between floors of establishment, using dumbwaiter.

77

TOOLROOM ATTENDANT

Receives, stores, and issues handtools, dies, and equipment, such as measuring devices, in industrial establishment: Keeps records of tools issued to and returned by workers. Searches for lost or misplaced tools. Prepares periodic inventory or keeps perpetual inventory and requisitions stock as needed. Unpacks and stores new equipment. Visually inspects tools or measures with micrometer for wear or defects and reports damaged and worn-out equipment to superiors. May coat tools with grease or other preservative, using brush or spray gun. May make minor tool repairs. May carry or deliver information by hand truck to workers. May attach identification tags or engrave identifying information on tools and equipment, using electric marking tool.

WAITER/WAITRESS

Serves food to patrons at counters and tables of coffee shops, lunchrooms, and other dining establishments: Presents menu, answers questions, and makes suggestions regarding food and service. Writes order on check or memorizes it. Relays order to kitchen and serves courses from kitchen or service bars. Observes guests to fulfill any additional request and to perceive when meal has been completed. Totals bill and accepts payment or refers patron to cashier. May ladle soup, toss salads, portion pies and desserts, brew coffee, and perform other services as determined by establishment's size and practices. May clear and reset counters or tables at conclusion of each course.

Answer Key

Building Success

· IN THE WORKPLACE ·

INTRODUCTION

Many people are unprepared for the demands made on them in the workplace. Such people may include experienced workers as well as first-time job seekers, students in job training programs, and people who have been long out of work or unable to hold a job for reasons they do not fully understand. These people may need information on some basic principles related to the world of work. Such principles include being on the job every day, being on time, getting along with others, following directions, and so on.

The stories in this book were taken from real-life situations. The problems the characters encounter were those the author found to be most common during many years of working with people in job placement and training. The successes and failures of the characters are typical too. Reading about how other people dealt with their job-related problems can help prepare students for their own career problems.

The situations are presented in a mixture of stories and socio-dramas. The socio-dramas allow students to role-play both the workers and the employers. This lets them see both sides of each situation. Several students should play the different roles. It is suggested that the same student play the worker in one socio-drama and the employer in another. The role-playing, along with discussions of what happens in the real work-a-day world, can help prepare students to meet similar situations in their own lives.

ANSWERS TO THE EXERCISES

Beat the Clock

Pages 2-3

A. Answers will vary.

B. 1. Others depend on them. **2.** Al. **3.** 7:30. **4.** So he would not be late. **5.** Answers will vary.

C. 1. Underline cord, curler, carnival, counter, cabinet, committee, and community. **2. a.** aide. **b.** cabinet. **c.** projector. **d.** alarm. **3. a.** their. **b.** came. **c.** did. **4. a.** showing. **b.** correcting. **c.** building. **d.** working.

All Right!

Pages 5-6

A. Answers will vary.

B. 1. He is doing very well. Thanked him for working overtime. He is early to work every day. Everyone seems to like him. **2.** It spoils the whole day. **3.** He didn't mind. It was part of his job. **4.** Yes. **5.** Ron takes an early bus just in case the bus might be running late. He doesn't want to be late for work.

C. 1. Answers will vary. **2. a.** every/one.

b. pay/day. **c.** some/thing. **d.** some/one. **e.** some/times. **f.** him/self. **g.** over/time. **h.** every/thing.

The Toolroom Mystery

Pages 8-9

A. Answers will vary.

B. 1. Ramona was working in the toolroom of a large car repair shop. **2.** Her job was to check out tools to the mechanics and check them in again when the mechanics were through with them. **3.** Many expensive tools were stolen. **4.** She let Joe borrow the key to the toolroom.

C. 1. a. costing a lot of money. **b.** examine closely. **2. a.** gave. **b.** brought. **c.** stole. **d.** made. **e.** broke. **f.** got. **3. a.** any/one. **b.** some/one. **c.** tool/room. **4.** borrow — lend, break — mend, lose — find, leave — take, friend — enemy, remember — forget.

Hurry Back

Pages 11-13

A. Answers will vary.

80

B. 1. Service station. **2.** He keeps talking to some customers and keeps other customers waiting. **3.** It was a time of day when there were few customers. **4.** Most people would rather get good service.

C. 1. Answers will vary. **2. a.** service. **b.** manage. **c.** check. **d.** work. **e.** regular. **f.** train. **g.** custom or customer. **h.** look. **3.** calling — calls, understands — understanding, suggestion — suggests, customers — customer, manager — manage, waiting — waits, worker — work, services — servicing, unfriendly — friendly, interested — interesting. **4.** Answers will vary. **5.** Answers will vary. **6.** Put gas in cars; check oil, battery, tires; change tires; wash car windows; sweep or wash the driveway.

Sweet Success

Pages 15-16

A. Answers will vary.

B. 1. He followed directions. He tried to do a good job. He was careful. **2.** He learned the numbers that belonged to each department. **3.** He was offered the job of being in charge of the loading dock. **4.** The job seemed awfully big to him. He wasn't sure he could do it.

C. 1. Answers will vary. **2. a.** classroom. **b.** stockroom. **c.** bedroom. **d.** bathroom. **3. a.** very good. **b.** all right, acceptable. **c.** raise in rank. **4.** Answers will vary.

A Look in the Mirror

Pages 18-19

A. Answers will vary.

B. 1. In a cafeteria. **2.** Sue's blouse had a button missing. It was wrinkled. Her skirt was pinned. Her hair was not combed. **3.** Answers will vary, but Sue is obviously young. **4.** She needed to learn to be neat in her appearance, personal habits, and with her clothes.

C. 1. Answers will vary. **2. a.** mirrors. **b.** uniforms. **c.** workers. **d.** friends. **3. a.** combing. **b.** trying. **c.** needing. **d.** missing. **4. a.** combed. **b.** disappointed. **c.** ironed. **d.** placed.

The Drop-in

Pages 21-22

A. Answers will vary.

B. 1. Most places will not hire Don because he is too young (under eighteen). **2.** Don has been able to get part-time work in a grocery store and a temporary job at a service station. **3.** Don told Chiang he wouldn't drop out of school if he were him. **4.** Chiang has been working in the automotive shop at school. **5.** Don is thinking of going back to school.

C. 1. a. seventeen. **b.** eighteen. **2. a.** a paper to be filled out by someone asking for a job. **b.** lasting. **c.** lasting for a short time. **d.** the time one must work. **3.** Answers will vary.

Just a Scratch

Pages 24-26

A. Answers will vary.

B. 1. Working in a florist shop. **2.** Cutting and fitting chicken wire into some planters. **3.** Gene did not like the chicken wire, as it scratched his hands. **4.** No. **5.** No. **6.** Answers will vary. **7.** Answers will vary.

C. 1. a. worry. **b.** run. **c.** break. **d.** suppose. **e.** stem. **f.** finish. **g.** order. **h.** scratch. **i.** scrub. **j.** learn. **2.** Answers will vary. **3. a.** carried. **b.** worried. **c.** hurried. **d.** applied. **e.** tried. **f.** dried. **g.** married. **h.** complied. **i.** supplied. **j.** curried. **4. a.** running. **b.** cutting. **c.** fitting. **d.** swimming. **e.** shopping. **f.** putting. **g.** shunning. **h.** spinning. **i.** flopping. **j.** slipping. **5. a.** helper. **b.** sprayer. **c.** owner. **d.** worker. **e.** planter. **f.** dancer. **g.** player. **h.** baker.

Time and Again

Pages 28-30

A. Answers will vary.
B. 1. Jewelry. **2.** Candy. **3.** Shop. **4.** Carol.

5. Get back from lunch on time, take care of her counter, forget about makeup on the job. **6.** Answers will vary. **7.** Each counter has its own problems. **8.** Answers will vary.

C. 1. a. one. **b.** two. **c.** three. **d.** four. **e.** five. **f.** six. **2. a.** some/times. **b.** every/where. **c.** every/thing. **d.** some/where. **e.** worth/while. **3. a.** lately. **b.** quickly. **c.** slowly. **d.** quietly. **e.** freely. **f.** loudly. **g.** shortly. **h.** unexpectedly. **i.** certainly. **j.** doubtfully. **4. a.** late. **b.** problem. **c.** check. **d.** remind (mind). **e.** arrange. **f.** mention. **g.** get. **h.** work. **i.** hard. **j.** do. **5. a.** never. **b.** seldom. **c.** unhappy. **d.** early. **e.** shorter. **f.** play. **g.** messy. **h.** dirty. **i.** awake. **j.** faster.

Too Proud to Apologize

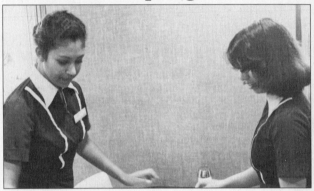

Pages 32-34

A. Answers will vary.

B. 1. Eighteen. **2.** In a large cafeteria. **3.** Pick up dirty dishes; take the dirty things to the kitchen on a cart; fill sugar bowls; pick up empty trays; and get extra coffee, tea, or water for customers. **4.** Answers may vary. **5.** Because the customers were listening to the argument. **6.** She didn't want to admit she was wrong. **7.** Mary quit her job.

C. 1. Answers will vary. **2. a.** fourteen. **b.** fifteen. **c.** sixteen. **d.** seventeen. **e.** eighteen. **f.** nineteen. **g.** thirteen. **h.** twelve. **i.** eleven. **j.** twenty. **3. a.** helpful. **b.** playful. **c.** careful. **d.** truthful. **e.** thankful. **f.** cheerful. **g.** doubtful. **h.** spiteful. **i.** forgetful. **j.** neglectful. **4. a.** I am. **b.** do not. **c.** she is. **d.** you are. **e.** that is. **f.** what is. **g.** they have. **h.** we will. **5. a.** won't. **b.** couldn't. **c.** doesn't. **d.** I'm. **e.** you're. **f.** he's. **g.** don't. **h.** you'll. **i.** she'll. **j.** he's. **k.** they've. **l.** she's.

Who's the Boss

Pages 36-37

A. Answers will vary.

B. 1. Answers will vary. **2.** Learn the importance of cooperation. **3.** Yes; no. **4.** Pete could have done as Mr. Walker asked. He could have asked Ms. Clay later if he had made the right decision.

C. 1. a. writing paper or supplies. **b.** one who helps another. **c.** rush; in a hurry. **d.** Several things, names, or numbers. **e.** a flat space to store things. **2.** Answers will vary. **3. a.** employing, employer. **b.** training, trainer. **c.** buying, buyer. **d.** working, worker. **e.** listening, listener. **f.** teaching, teacher. **4. a.** one, first. **b.** two, second. **c.** three, third. **d.** four, fourth. **e.** five, fifth.

One Chance Too Many

Pages 39-40

A. Answers will vary.

B. 1. Part-time. **2.** Afternoons. **3.** Dolores stood on a box instead of a stepladder. **4.** She should have gone after the stepladder. **5.** She hurt her ankle.

C. 1. a. ask. **b.** need. **c.** climb. **d.** borrow. **e.** safe. **f.** rule. **g.** surprise. **h.** decide. **i.** work. **j.** box. **k.** slip. **l.** tip. **2. a.** has done, have done. **b.** has watched, have watched. **c.** has gone, have gone. **d.** has wanted, have wanted. **e.** has fallen, have fallen. **f.** has baked, have baked. **3. a.** higher, highest. **b.** slower, slowest. **c.** faster, fastest.

The Whistler

Pages 42-44

A. Answers will vary.

B. 1. In a hotel coffee shop. **2.** Table setter. **3.** Whistling. **4.** Jim went to the kitchen to sing and dance and have fun. **5.** Yes. **6.** Answers will vary.

C. 1. Answers will vary. **2. a.** 6. **b.** 11. **c.** 15. **d.** 12. **e.** 17. **f.** 4. **3. a.** their. **b.** there. **c.** Their. **4. a.** get. **b.** do. **c.** train. **d.** whistle. **e.** work. **f.** go. **g.** appoint. **h.** manage. **i.** break. **j.** neglect. **5. a.** talks. **b.** classmates. **c.** habits. **d.** appointments. **e.** workers. **f.** customers. **g.** acts. **h.** teachers. **6.** Answers will vary.

Too Many Excuses

Pages 46-47

A. Answers will vary.

B. 1. At a factory. **2.** He refused to work overtime. **3.** He wanted to leave early every Friday. He complained about money taken out of his paycheck for being late. He didn't go to work one day when it was raining. **4.**

Extra money was taken out of Bill's pay because he was late. **5.** Answers will vary. **6.** Bill and Doris worked at the bakery at the same time. **7.** Answers may vary, but if anybody chooses Bill, you should have another discussion of maturity.

C. 1. a. silly. **b.** found fault. **c.** person who directs the work of others. **2.** Answers will vary.

Just Joking

Pages 49-50

A. Answers will vary.

B. 1. See the "Dictionary of Job Descriptions" at the back of the student's book. **2.** Something that is being offered at a lower price than normal. **3.** He played a joke on someone while both should have been working. **4.** Yes; Dave was angry. He said, "Some joke. What are you trying to do? You want to get me fired?" **5.** Answers will vary.

C. 1. a. shelves. **b.** leaves. **c.** halves. **d.** loaves. **2. a.** work. **b.** display. **c.** customer. **d.** decide. **e.** ask. **f.** box. **g.** grin. **h.** quick. **3.** Answers will vary.

Time for a Change

Pages 52-54

A. Answers will vary.

B. 1. Nell got nervous when Charles was around. **2.** Six months. **3.** Her hand shook; she forgot some orders; sometimes she mixed up her orders. **4.** No. **5.** No. **6.** Nell was not nervous anymore.

C. 1. a. Nell was polite. **b.** Are you bothered? **c.** She left a tip for the woman who waited on her. **2. a.** nineteen. **b.** six. **c.** twenty. **d.** fifteen. **3.** January — Jan., February — Feb., March — Mar., April — Apr., May — May, June — June, July — July, August — Aug., September — Sept., October — Oct., November — Nov., December — Dec. **4. a.** lunch/time. **b.** every/one. **c.** lunch/room. **d.** down/town. **e.** up/set. **f.** every/body. **g.** boy/friend. **h.** any/thing. **i.** some/times. **5. a.** here. **b.** too. **c.** I. **d.** two. **e.** her. **f.** him.

More Fun Than Work

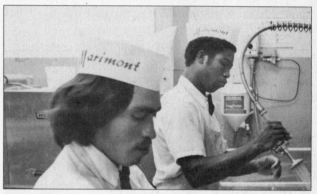

Pages 56-57

A. Answers will vary.

B. 1. Dishwasher. **2.** He popped Tom with a towel, argued with the elevator operator, cursed one of the cooks, threw a biscuit, and hid in the laundry room. **3.** Yes; first paragraph. **4.** For a day or two, but it didn't last. **5.** George needs to learn to be serious.

C. 1. a. moving belt. **b.** control. **2. a.** longer — longest. **b.** smarter — smartest. **c.** busier — busiest. **d.** harder — hardest. **e.** sorrier — sorriest. **3. a.** more, most. **b.** more, most. **c.** more, most.

Slow but Sure

Pages 59-61

A. Answers will vary.

B. 1. Delivers the mail. **2.** So everyone will be able to plan their work. **3.** No. She wanted to help Amy do her job better. **4.** She wanted Amy to keep working there. **5.** After work, at lunch, or at break time.

C. 1. Answers will vary. **2. a.** worked. **b.** decided. **c.** helped. **d.** pushed. **e.** explained. **f.** talked. **g.** finished. **h.** sorted. **3. a.** did. **b.** left. **c.** had. **d.** forgot. **e.** said. **f.** thought. **g.** went. **h.** bought. **i.** cried. **j.** drove. **k.** dug. **l.** dove. **4. a.** 30 minutes. **b.** 15 minutes. **c.** 60 minutes. **d.** 90 minutes. **e.** 120 minutes. **f.** 135 minutes. **5. a.** explain. **b.** complain. **c.** friend. **d.** be. **e.** stop. **f.** deliver. **g.** deliver. **h.** work. **i.** work. **j.** like.

Reading Is the Key

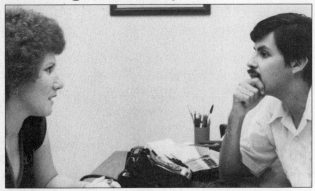

Pages 63-64

A. Answers will vary.

B. 1. Six out of these: set the table, clear the table, scrape the dishes, wash windows, dust venetian blinds, empty wastebaskets, dust the furniture, clean the bathrooms. **2.** 8. **3.** She could not read it. **4.** She was ashamed to let anyone know she couldn't read. **5.** She could have told her boss about her reading problem.

C. 1. a. a paper with things to do or remember written on it. **b.** rub off. **c.** dump out. **d.** jobs. **2.** Answers will vary.

The Last Detail

Pages 66-68

A. Answers will vary.

B. 1. In a school cafeteria. **2.** Beverly takes trays of salads and desserts from the refrigerator to the counter and takes the empty trays back to the kitchen. **3.** Beverly is careless about keeping her hands and fingernails clean and looking right. **4.** No; Beverly guessed what Ms. Smith was going to say. **5.** Beverly decided to take better care of her hands and nails. **6.** No, because she wanted to keep her job and followed suggestions to improve her habits.

C. 1. a. understand clearly. **b.** careful listening or watching. **c.** way of thinking, acting, or feeling. **d.** not thinking or watching what you do or say. **2. a.** playing. **b.** working. **c.** planting. **d.** keeping. **e.** following. **f.** being. **3.** clean — dirty, follow — lead, late — early, remember — forget, careless — careful, morning — evening, work — play. **4. a.** unfolded. **b.** unimportant. **c.** unhappy. **d.** unclean. **e.** unfinished. **f.** uncovered. **5. a.** like. **b.** follow. **c.** napkin. **d.** mean. **e.** complain. **f.** pull. **g.** look. **h.** chip. **i.** hand **j.** leave. **k.** sit. **l.** serve. **6.** Monday — Mon., Tuesday — Tues., Wednesday — Wed., Thursday — Thur., Friday — Fri.

WORK ATTITUDES PRESENTED

in *Building Success in the Workplace*

Lesson Title	Job Success Issues Presented	Lesson Title	Job Success Issues Presented
Beat the Clock	Importance of being on time and the need to cooperate in relationships with co-workers.	**Who's the Boss**	Cooperating with your supervisor and willingly learning to understand the job and follow directions.
All Right!	Dependability and the desire to do a job well.	**One Chance Too Many**	Understanding safety rules and using these rules on the job.
The Toolroom Mystery	Being trustworthy and carefully placing trust in co-workers.	**The Whistler**	Learning what behavior is appropriate for the job.
Hurry Back	Desire to do the job well and willingness to take suggestions.	**Too Many Excuses**	Accepting responsibility for your actions — this means mistakes as well as successes.
Sweet Success	Willingness to accept responsibility and willingness to accomplish more than is required of the job.	**Just Joking**	Learning what is expected of you in the workplace and taking the appropriate action in every situation.
A Look in the Mirror	The importance of personal grooming and appearance in the workplace.	**Time for a Change**	Consideration for others and helping them build success in their workplace.
The Drop-in	Understanding the importance and advantages of education.	**More Fun Than Work**	Self discipline on the job.
Just a Scratch	Knowing how your own abilities match up with job requirements.	**Slow but Sure**	Willingness to follow a schedule and understanding the job requirements.
Time and Again	Being on time and conscientiously doing a good job.	**Reading Is the Key**	Asking for explanations when directions are not clear and stating your own job qualifications clearly.
Too Proud To Apologize	Controlling your temper and doing a job well.	**The Last Detail**	Importance of personal appearance in the workplace.